Visitor's Guide

# Visitor's Guide

Trinidad de Antonio

MUSEO NACIONAL DEL PRADO

## Introduction

The Prado Museum was inaugurated on 19 November 1819 by Ferdinand VII, who had inherited the paintings from his forebears, most of the Spanish monarchs having been collectors of some importance and considerable enthusiasm. In 1872, shortly after becoming the property of the Spanish State, the Museum was enriched with a number of works, mostly religious, from the Museo de la Trinidad. This museum had been established in 1836 to display works of art from those ecclesiastical institutions that had been closed and their patrimony appropriated by the government. Finally, the museum received an important set of nineteenth century Spanish works in 1971 from the defunct Museum of Modern Art, and many additional works have been purchased or donated.

Owing to the nature of its origins, the Prado will never be an encyclopaedic museum with the capacity to display the full panorama of the history of painting. It is, on the other hand, highly representative of the tastes of the Spanish monarchs and of the evolution of Spanish history and art. It is, above all, the essential museum for all those wishing to see the works of some of the greatest painters of all time, such as El Greco, Velázquez, Goya, Bosch, Rubens and Titian. The Prado's origins also account for the uneven representation of schools and artists in its collections.

Qualitatively and quantitatively, Spanish painting is best represented, followed by the Flemish and Italian schools – an evident reflection of the country's aesthetic and political interests over the centuries. French art is also in evidence, especially from the period after the accession to the Spanish throne of the Bourbon dynasty in the eighteenth century. On the other hand, Dutch, German and English works are scant, owing to the more distant relations between these countries and Spain during the period when the collections were growing.

The extraordinary quality of its pictures, and its historical and artistic pre-eminence in the context of European art, has turned the Prado into one of the most important museums in the world. It has also made a notable contribution to contemporary art, since its opening allowed the hitherto little-known Spanish School to be discovered and appreciated by public and artists alike. The art of Velázquez influenced Manet and the beginnings of French Impressionism; the early years of Picasso can be explained only by his knowledge of El Greco; and Goya was a fundamental figure for many twentieth-century artists. This is why the Prado's galleries inevitably draw all those with an interest in art and beauty, be they painters, scholars or art lovers in general.

FRA ANGELICO

## *The Annunciation*

c. 1426. Gold and tempera on panel,
194 x 194 cm. P15

This altarpiece was painted for the
Convent of San Domenico in Fie-
sole, near Florence. The main scene
is set inside a Renaissance portico
and represents the Annunciation:
the announcement by the archangel
Gabriel to Mary that she would bear
the son of God. On the left is the
expulsion of Adam and Eve from
Paradise, and episodes of the Life
of the Virgin are narrated in the pre-
della panels below. Fra Angelico
dedicated his work exclusively to
religious subjects believing that
works of art should be acts of religious devotion. His style is a blend
of Gothic – as evinced by his use of
gold and the linear design of the
folds – combined with the new Renaissance concern with defining spa-
tial depth.

# ANDREA MANTEGNA

## *The Death of the Virgin*

c. 1462. Tempera on panel,
54.5 x 42 cm. P248

Mantegna represents the dying Virgin Mary surrounded by the apostles. The upper part of the panel originally showed Christ receiving the Virgin's soul in heaven and this section is preserved at the National Art Gallery of Ferrara. The composition is dominated by the artist's concern with perspective and the convincing representation of a three dimensional space. The tiled floor recedes to the group of figures beneath the window, the centre of which acts as a 'vanishing point'. Through the window can be seen the lagoon of Mantua, a city ruled by the Gonzaga family, whose service Mantegna entered in 1459. This view is one of the first topographically recognisable landscapes in Italian painting.

ANTONELLO DA MESSINA

## *The Dead Christ Supported by an Angel*

c. 1475-1476. Oil and tempera on panel, 74 x 51 cm. P3092

Antonello's figures are sharply delineated against the bright background depicting Messina, the artist's birthplace. Trained in Naples, Antonello also became familiar with the technical virtuosity of Netherlandish painting, demonstrated in his meticulous treatment of tiny details such as Christ's hair, and the landscape in the background. This Northern influence coexists with characteristics of the Italian school, such as his handling of the monumentality of shapes and of background depth. The iconography and emotional treatment of the subject are related to the work of Giovanni Bellini, whose paintings he encountered on a trip to Venice in 1475.

BARTOLOMÉ BERMEJO

## *Saint Dominic of Silos enthroned as Abbot*

1474-1477. Oil on panel,
242 x 130 cm. P1323

This panel was painted for the high altar of the parish church of Daroca, Saragossa, and represents Saint Dominic, an eleventh-century Benedictine Abbot who founded the Monastery of Silos in Burgos. The abbot appears dressed as a bishop, sitting on a Gothic throne, adorned with polychrome images of the three theological virtues: Faith, Hope and Charity; and four cardinal virtues: Prudence, Justice, Fortitude and Temperance. Set on a gold background, typical of the medieval period, the painting is outstanding for its monumentality and for the intense realism of the face, an aspect of the influence of Netherlandish art on Bermejo.

5

ROGER VAN DER WEYDEN

*Descent from the Cross*

c. 1435. Oil on panel,
220 x 262 cm. P2825

Van der Weyden made this painting
for the Crossbowmen's Chapel of
the Church of Notre-Dame in Lou-
vain. It is one of his best-known
works due to its masterly composition, its technical virtuosity and its
size. The ten figures are almost life-
size, which is uncommon in Netherlandish painting. The artist creates
an intensely dramatic scene. Break-
ing away from the usual vertical for-
mat of Descents from the Cross,
Van der Weyden focuses on the Virgin Mary's grief for her dead son.
She faints into the arms of Saint
John as Joseph of Arimathea and
Nicodemus lower the body of Christ
from the cross.

HANS MEMLING

## Triptych of the Adoration of the Magi

c. 1479-1480. Oil on panel,
central panel: 96 × 147.5 cm;
wing panels: 98 × 63 cm. P1557

Although today these three scenes of *The Nativity, The Adoration of the Magi* and *The Purification* are displayed in a single frame, they were originally created as a folding triptych. They were painted by Memling in the Flemish city of Bruges, where he settled after completing his training with Roger Van der Weyden in Brussels. His models and compositions are drawn from his master, while the strong verticals and his interest in light and landscape recall the works of Jan van Eyck (c. 1390-1441). From these influences, Memling, who was German, defined an original, harmonious and balanced style, characterised by a clear definition of space and brilliant colours.

HIERONYMUS BOSCH

## Table of the Seven Deadly Sins

Late fifteenth century. Oil on panel,
120 x 150 cm. P2822

This panel was purchased by Philip II, who displayed it in the monastery of El Escorial. Considered one of the painter's early works, it has four small roundels in the corners depicting the Four Last Things: Death, Judgment, Heaven and Hell; and a larger circle with an image of Christ in the centre like an eye. The outer ring shows scenes from daily life illustrating the Seven Deadly Sins. The Latin inscription next to the image of Jesus emphasises the moral content of the work: 'Beware, Beware, God is Watching'. Jesus is represented as the Man of Sorrows to remind us that his death redeemed mankind from sin.

HIERONYMUS BOSCH

## The Garden of Earthly Delights

1500-1505. Oil on panel, 220 x 389 cm. P2823

Bosch's highly original paintings, filled with symbolic images difficult to interpret, were hugely admired in sixteenth-century Spain. This triptych, painted late in his career, is one of his most enigmatic and beautiful creations. Closed, it shows the third day of Creation; while open, it shows the Earthly Paradise on the left panel and Hell on the right. The Garden of Delights occupies the central panel, a world given over to pleasure and sin, especially lust, painted with the meticulous realism characteristic of the Netherlandish school. Bosch's intention was to represent the ephemeral nature of earthly delights and their ill-fated consequences.

## JOACHIM PATINIR

### *Crossing the Styx*

c. 1520-1524. Oil on panel,
64 x 103 cm. P1616

Patinir was the first European artist
to specialise in painting landscapes
and can therefore be considered
the father of the genre. His style
combines fantasy and realism and
he shows a special skill for painting the immensity and beauty of
nature. According to Greek mythology, Charon transported the souls
of the dead across the River Styx
towards Hell. Patinir Christianises
the subject, making it a choice
between good and evil. On the left,
angels point towards the path to
Paradise, while on the right, the
gatekeeper, Cerberus, a three-head-
ed dog, guards the gates to Hell in a
gloomy landscape that contrasts
with the clarity of the sky.

# PIETER BRUEGHEL THE ELDER

## *The Triumph of Death*

c. 1562. Oil on panel, 117 x 162 cm. P1393

Inspired by the literary theme of the Dance of Death, Brueghel painted this work in a manner reminiscent of Bosch. He creates a broad panorama, the elevated position of the horizon allowing for the representation of a distressing and macabre spectacle in which Death, mounted on a horse, leads a large army of skeletons to destroy the world of the living. The predominately red palette emphasizes the devastation. The figure of Death, who is meticulously and realistically depicted, makes no distinction between gender, age, or social class.

## ALBRECHT DÜRER

### *Self Portrait*

1498. Oil on panel, 52 x 41 cm. P2179

Written in German on the window sill are the words: '1498. I painted this after my own image. I was twenty-six years old. *Albrecht Dürer*'. This inscription and the image itself show Dürer's desire for this work to exalt his persona and his art. It is a self-portrait depicting a distinguished and proud figure, richly attired, and it is painted with an extraordinary level of technical virtuosity. Perhaps Dürer wanted to defend the painter's social standing and his status as an intellectually creative artist, rather than a mere craftsman, which is how painters were still considered in many European countries.

# ALBRECHT DÜRER

## *Adam and Eve*

1507. Oil on panel, 209 x 81 cm.
P2177 and P2178

Dürer's representations of Adam and Eve reflect his interest in the nude and in human proportions, a subject on which he wrote several theoretical works. They also illustrate his knowledge of classic Italian Renaissance art, which he would have studied during his two trips to Venice. The idealisation of these figures – the first life-size nudes in German painting – are in contrast, stylistically, to Dürer's nothern training, with its interest in naturalism and detail. Both paintings were given to Philip IV as a gift by Queen Christina of Sweden.

13

ANTHONIS MOR
## Queen Mary Tudor
1554. Oil on panel, 109 x 84 cm. P2108

Mary Tudor, born in 1516, was the only daughter of Henry VIII and his first wife, Catherine of Aragon. Once Henry had divorced Catherine, Mary was considered illegitimate and expelled from the court. In 1553, after the death of her stepbrother Edward VI, she ascended the throne of England and restored Catholicism. In 1554 she made a political marriage to Philip II but died without issue in 1558. Mor presents her richly dressed, in accordance with her status, and holding a red rose, the symbol of the Tudor dynasty, in her right hand. Employing the descriptive style of Netherlandish painting, the artist creates a masterpiece of majestic dignity without excessively idealising Mary's less than beautiful face.

RAPHAEL

# The Cardinal

c. 1510. Oil on panel, 79 x 61 cm. P299

Shortly after arriving in Rome, Raphael painted this portrait, which probably shows Cardinal Francesco Alidosi, who was assassinated in 1511. Raphael painted relatively few independent portraits while in the Eternal City, but he left some memorable examples in his Vatican frescoes. For this composition, he seems to have been inspired by Leonardo da Vinci's *Mona Lisa,* since he chose a similar pyramidal composition, defined by the body and position of the arm. However, Raphael preferred a neutral background that enhances the physical presence of the sitter. This image has become the archetype of a prince of the Renaissance church.

15

## RAPHAEL
### Madonna of the Fish

1513-1514. Oil on panel, transferred
to canvas, 215 x 158 cm. P297

This altar painting is a *sacra conver-
sazione,* an image of the Virgin Mary
with the baby Jesus, accompanied
by several saints, a typical composition of the Italian Renaissance. This
work was painted for the monastery
of San Domenico in Naples. To the
right is Saint Jerome, dressed as a
cardinal with the lion that accompanied him during his stay in the
desert, and reading the Bible, which
he translated into Latin. On the left
are the archangel Raphael and
Tobias, who holds the fish whose
bile healed his father's blindness.
The work has the clear composition
and harmonious balance of form
and colour characteristic of Raphael's artistic ability, as well as the
ideal beauty of his figures.

TITIAN

# Bacchanal of the Andrians

1523-1526. Oil on canvas,
175 x 193 cm. P418

One of Titian's first successes outside Venice was the decoration of the *camerino d'alabastro* of Alfonso I d'Este in Ferrara, which included this *Bacchanal,* the *Worship of Venus,* (also at the Prado Museum) and *Bacchus and Ariadne* (at the National Gallery, London). The scene is inspired by the *Imagines* of Philostratus, a Greek text of the third century B.C., which describes famous paintings of Antiquity. The scene shows the effects of wine on gods and men during a celebration honouring Bacchus, god of wine, on the Island of Andros. The luminosity and chromatic richness that dominate the picture are characteristic of Titian.

TITIAN

## *Charles V at Mühlberg*

1548. Oil on canvas, 335 x 283 cm. P410

This equestrian portrait is the best-known painting of a Habsburg ruler and one of the most famous portraits in the history of art. It was painted by Titian in Augsburg in 1548 to commemorate the Emperor's victory over the Protestant forces on 24 April 1547 at the Battle of Mühlberg, on the banks of the River Elbe. The composition was inspired by the equestrian statue of Emperor Marcus Aurelius in Rome and the print of *The Horse and Death* by Albrecht Dürer. The painter chose not to use overtly allegorical imagery, but to show Charles V as a Christian knight, defender of the faith, and heir to the Roman Imperial tradition.

TITIAN

## *Danaë and the Shower of Gold*

1553. Oil on canvas,
129.8 x 181.2 cm. P425

This sensual painting of *Danaë* is highly representative of the Venetian ideal of beauty. It is one of a series of paintings known as 'poesie' that Titian created for Philip II. Based on ancient literary texts, particularly Ovid's *Metamorphoses,* the poesie were designed purely to delight the senses, without requiring allegorical or moral interpretation. Danaë was the daughter of King Acrisius who had been warned in a prophecy that he would die by the hand of his grandson. In an attempt to avoid his fate, he imprisoned his daughter in a tower but the resourceful Zeus transformed himself into a shower of gold in order to reach her. Their son Perseus was to fulfill the prophecy.

TINTORETTO

*Christ Washing the Disciples' Feet*

1548-1549. Oil on canvas, 210 x 533 cm. P2824

This scene represents the episode immediately before the Last Supper when Jesus washed the feet of Saint Peter as an example of humility. Tintoretto demonstrates his compositional skill and the ability to narrate a story that turned him into one of the leading painters of large-scale religious works in Venice. The positioning of the main characters responds to the paint-ing's original location – a side wall of the presbytery of the Venetian church of San Marcuola – and they are placed deliberately close to the parishioners. The coherence of the painting's composition is best understood by looking at it from the right and following the diagonal line that begins next to the figure of Christ and extends to the background arch of the canal.

VERONESE

# Venus and Adonis

c. 1580. Oil on canvas, 162 x 191 cm. P482

Adonis rests upon the lap of Venus, who fans his face while looking at Cupid who is holding off a hound. The work illustrates a passage from Ovid's *Metamorphoses* recounting a love destroyed by the sudden death of one of the lovers. Veronese chooses the couple's last moment of happiness before Adonis is killed by the boar. Tragedy is announced by twilight invading the scene, and the troubled face of Venus, foretelling the fate awaiting her lover. It is typical of Veronese to use such a contrasting range of colours dominated by oranges, blues and greens. The importance he gives to the landscape is characteristic of his late work.

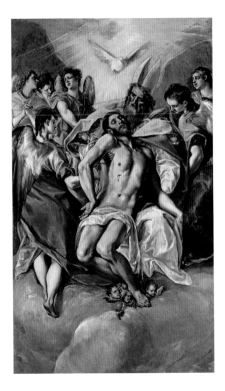

## EL GRECO

### *The Holy Trinity*

1577-1579. Oil on canvas,
300 x 179 cm. P824

This is one of the first works painted by El Greco in Spain. His early style was influenced by his familiarity with Venetian colours and Roman design. He uses a range of tones similar to Tintoretto and defines his monumental figures in a vigorous style that recalls Michelangelo, particularly in the anatomy of Jesus whose body is supported by God the Father wearing an oriental mitre. The composition, with the angels and the dove signifying the Holy Spirit, was inspired by a Dürer engraving. The angels' expressions of suffering allude to the sacrifice made by Christ to save humanity.

EL GRECO

## *The Adoration of the Shepherds*

1612-1614. Oil on canvas,
319 x 180 cm. P2988

Destined for his tomb in the church of Santo Domingo el Antiguo in Toledo, this painting is one of the last works created by El Greco. The entire composition revolves around the Infant Christ lying on a white cloth and radiating light. The nighttime scene with its sharp contrasts between light and dark is a response to the prevalence of chiaroscuro in early-seventeenth-century painting; but the broken brushstrokes and elongated figures are distinctively El Greco's. Their expressive gestures and the visual distortion of their anatomy are characteristic of the artist's late work.

EL GRECO

## *Knight with his Hand on his Chest*

c. 1580. Oil on canvas, 81.8 x 65.8 cm. P809

This unknown gentleman was clearly a knight since he wears a sword and a fine gold chain and medallion. The way his hand is placed on his chest may indicate that he is swearing an oath. Portrait painting, as a genre, began during the Renaissance and was employed in the service of those in political power. By the end of the sixteenth century, however, El Greco began to create images of members of the new civil and urban society in Toledo, and this work is one of the earliest examples. In it one can appreciate the warm naturalism and visual impact of light that the young El Greco had absorbed during his training in Venice.

CARAVAGGIO

## *David Victorious over Goliath*

1600-1605. Oil on canvas,
110 x 91 cm. P65

This episode from the Old Testament constitutes part of the last battle between the Philistines and the Israelines. The young shepherd, David, killed Goliath, the Philistine champion, using only his sling. David appears kneeling over his defeated enemy, tying his hair to a cord in order to carry the head as a trophy. Caravaggio, with his characteristic naturalism, doesn't paint a hero, but a composed youth who has beaten his opponent thanks to his adroitness and divine assistance. The theatrical lighting makes the scene more dramatic and emphasizes the main lines of the composition.

## NICOLAS POUSSIN

### *Parnassus*

1630-1631. Oil on canvas, 145 x 197 cm. P2313

Parnassus is the mountain where, according to Greek mythology, Apollo lived with the nine Muses, the daughters of Zeus, who were the protectors of poetry, art and science. The French painter, Poussin, was particularly interested in classical art and culture and this work was inspired by the Vatican fresco of the same subject by Raphael. It represents Apollo, with a nude torso, surrounded by the Muses with their respective attributes. Apollo is offering the nectar of the gods to Homer who is being crowned with laurels by Calliope, the muse of epic poetry. The scene is observed by other poets and artists, also wearing laurel crowns as a symbol of their fame.

JUSEPE DE RIBERA

## *Jacob's Dream*

1639. Oil on canvas, 179 x 233 cm. P1117

In the book of Genesis, the patri-
arch Jacob dreams of a ladder with
angels climbing up and down it. The
dream symbolises the ascent toward
God through spiritual perfection.
Ribera uses the language of realism
to represent the scene, emphasis-
ing the physical presence of the
dreamer. His solid figure contrasts
with the light brushstrokes of the
luminous ladder, which blends into
the golden sky above Jacob's head.
In this highly original composition,
the celestial vision is a mere sugges-
tion compared to the materiality of
Jacob. The strong horizontal of his
sleeping body is further extended
by the volume of the tree trunk.

### JUAN SÁNCHEZ COTÁN

## *Still Life with Game, Fruit and Vegetables*

1602. Oil on canvas, 68 x 89 cm. P7612

Although very few still lifes by Sánchez Cotán are known, this painter from Toledo defined the characteristics of the genre during the Baroque period. The model he created held sway with few variations until well into the seventeenth century. As in the case of this painting, his works are sober in appearance, with a select number of simple, natural components – fowl, vegetables and fruits – arranged on a window sill and depicted with meticulous draughtsmanship and precise modelling. An intense light heightens the plasticity of the forms against the dark background, achieving an extraordinary realism.

FRANCISCO DE ZURBARÁN

*Still Life with four vassels*

c. 1660. Oil on canvas,
46 x 84 cm. P2803

Zurbarán painted very few still lifes, but this one in particular is often cited as a prototype for the Spanish Golden Age. Lined up on a shelf are four vessels, the distinctive texture of each object highlighted against the dark background by the intense luminosity. It is the quality of light that is the protagonist of the work, defining the colour and volume of each individual object. The composition is uncomplicated, as is usual in Spanish still lifes, and illustrates the appreciation of simplicity and geometrical rigour that characterise the work of this Extremaduran painter.

FRANCISCO DE ZURBARÁN

## *Apparition of the Apostle Saint Peter to Saint Peter Nolasco*

1629. Oil on canvas, 179 x 223 cm. P1237

This work was painted by Zurbarán for the convent of La Merced in Seville to celebrate the canonisation in 1628 of Saint Peter Nolasco, the founder of the order. It represents one of the best-known episodes in the Saint's life – the miraculous apparition of the apostle Saint Peter, crucified, in his cell – in a simple, realistic language that communicates an intense spirituality. The artist focuses entirely on the solid presence of the figures without defining the space they occupy. The almost tactile quality of the fabrics is rendered with dense and precise brushwork.

DIEGO VELÁZQUEZ

## *The Drinkers*

1628-1629. Oil on canvas,
165 x 225 cm. P1170

This depiction of a young Bacchus celebrating with his companions is Velázquez's first mythological painting. It is extremely unusual in that the artist does not ennoble his mythological subjects but chooses a realistic interpretation with a certain picaresque irony, in keeping with the Spanish Baroque tradition. The scene displays the naturalist leanings typical of his early style, especially in the individualised treatment of the figures, but light here plays an important role. The dark backgrounds of Tenebrist painting are here relinquished thanks to the influence of sixteenth-century Venetian painting, which the artist had seen in the royal collection.

DIEGO VELÁZQUEZ

## *The Surrender of Breda*

1635. Oil on canvas, 307 x 367 cm. P1172

Ambrogio de Spinola, the Genoese general in command of the Spanish troops, is presented by Governor Justin of Nassau with the keys to the Dutch city of Breda, conquered after a long siege on 5 June 1625. Velázquez painted this episode for the Hall of Realms in the Buen Retiro Palace in Madrid. With elegance and generosity, Spinola avoids humiliating the vanquished in order to emphasise the clemency of the Spanish monarchy. The lances of the triumphant Spaniards separate the foreground from the distant landscape. With admirable fluidity and a skilful gradation of colours, the painter here achieves an impressive effect of atmospheric depth.

DIEGO VELÁZQUEZ

## The Buffoon Don Diego de Acedo, 'El Primo'

1635. Oil on canvas, 107 x 82 cm. P1201

Portraits of dwarfs and buffoons were common in Habsburg Spain. Velázquez painted realistic portraits of some of the 'men of pleasure' of the Madrid court, valuing their humanity without baulking at their deformity. This painting is a case in point. Don Diego de Acedo was a court official charged with the care of the seal bearing the king's signature, and this accounts for the objects around him. His nickname, *'El Primo'* (The Cousin), may allude to some family relationship with the painter himself, or may refer to a title bestowed by the king on a few noblemen who enjoyed the privilege of remaining with their heads covered while in his presence.

DIEGO VELÁZQUEZ

## *Las Meninas*

c. 1656. Oil on canvas,
318 x 276 cm. P1174

The composition of this work hinges on the Infanta Margarita, who is accompanied by several servants, including her maids of honour or *"meninas"*, whilst the image of her parents, Philip IV and Mariana of Austria, is reflected in the background mirror. Velázquez inserts the figures into precisely articulated planes of depth defined by light, which sharpens or softens the forms and creates an optical illusion of air and space with consummate skill. The apparent spontaneity of the scene contrasts with the difficult interpretation of its meaning. This may be related to the vindication of painting as a noble art, which would explain the presence of the self-portrait of the artist at work with his brushes.

DIEGO VELÁZQUEZ

## The Spinners

c. 1657. Oil on canvas,
220 x 289 cm. P1173

Velázquez took his inspiration from a mythological story in Ovid's *Metamorphoses*. According to the Roman author, Arachne, proud of her skill as a weaver, dared to challenge Minerva. Angered by her presumption, the goddess punished her by changing her into a spider. In the far background one can see the helmeted goddess is raising her arm over the young woman in a gesture of punishment. The story takes place in an everyday setting, perhaps inspired by the tapestry factory of Santa Isabel. The painter combines visual realism and the intellectual concept behind the myth with great mastery.

BARTOLOMÉ ESTEBAN
MURILLO

*The Patrician's Dream*

c. 1663. Oil on canvas,
232 x 522 cm. P994

This picture is inspired by the legend of the foundation of the Roman basilica of Santa Maria Maggiore, and was commissioned for the church of Santa María la Blanca in Seville. It shows the apparition of the Virgin to a fourth-century Roman patrician and his wife while they sleep, in which she makes known that a church should be dedicated to her upon the Es-quiline Hill. It is one of Murillo's most important works, owing to its technical quality and the beauty of its light effects; and also because of its masterly resolution of the pictorial narrative in the intimate and familiar style endorsed by the Catholic Church in the seventeenth century for religious scenes.

BARTOLOMÉ ESTEBAN
MURILLO

## *The Immaculate Conception*

c. 1678. Oil on canvas,
274 x 190 cm. P2809

Painted for the hospital of Los Venerables in Seville, this work was taken to France during the War of Independence by Marshal Soult and remained in his possession for some time before going to the Musée du Louvre. It was shown there for nearly a century before its final admittance to the Prado Museum in 1941. Murillo's fame is closely linked with this subject, which he painted a great many times, successfully reflecting the fervent devotion of the Spanish people to the Marian cult. In his sweet and delicate language, he created dynamic scenes like this one, which is typical of the artist at the height of his powers.

PETER PAUL RUBENS

*The Adoration of the Magi*

1609 and 1628. Oil on canvas,
353 x 496 cm. P1638

Rubens created this work in 1609
for the Town Hall of Antwerp. In
1618 the city offered it as a gift to
the Spanish minister Don Rodrigo
Calderón, whose possessions passed
to Philip IV after his death. When
the Flemish painter visited Spain in
1628, he re-encountered the picture
and modified it, repainting it with a
more fluid technique and enlarging
the composition with the addition
of a strip of canvas with Titianesque
angels at the top, and another on
the right in which he portrays himself on horseback. The result makes
it possible to appreciate the evolution of his technique, from the mus-
cular nudes and lighting contrasts
he learnt during his years of training
in Italy, to the theatrical dynamism
of his maturity.

## PETER PAUL RUBENS
### *The Three Graces*
c. 1635. Oil on panel, 221 x 181 cm. P1670

The daughters of Zeus and Eurynome were known as Aglaia, Euphrosyne and Thalia, or the Three Graces. They were at the service of Aphrodite, the goddess of love, and represented affability, sympathy and kindness. Rubens was inspired by Raphael, who had painted the same subject, although Rubens employs a more dynamic and theatrical style and introduces his own exuberant and sensual concept of female beauty. The figure on the left is recognisable as his second wife, Helena Fourment, whom he married shortly before painting this picture. It could be seen as a hymn to conjugal love, since it remained the painter's personal property until his death in 1640. It was later acquired by Philip IV at a sale of the artist's goods.

ANTHONY VAN DYCK

## Self Portrait with Sir Endymion Porter

c. 1635. Oil on canvas, 119 x 144 cm. P1489

Porter, the friend and protector of Van Dyck, was the Duke of Buckingham's secretary and a great art lover. What makes this dual portrait so exceptional is the visual significance of the composition. The different social ranks of the protagonists are distinguished by the colouring of their garments and the position of the sitters – white and facing front for the aristocrat, black and in profile for the artist. Their mutual affection is expressed by the positioning of their hands on the rock symbolising the strength of their friendship. Van Dyck painted this picture during his last years when he had become the principal portraitist at the English court.

REMBRANDT VAN RIJN

## *Artemisia*

1634. Oil on canvas,
143 x 154.7 cm. P2132

This painting probably represents Artemisia preparing to drink the dissolved ashes of Mausolus, her dead husband, from a goblet. It has occasionally also been interpreted as Sophonisba, the daughter of the Carthaginian general Hasdrubal and wife of Masinissa, who poisoned herself to avoid falling victim to Scipio's lust. Either way the subject is related to the exaltation of conjugal love, and was perhaps chosen by the painter in celebration of his marriage to Saskia van Uylenburch, his model for the work. Painted during a period of considerable success and happiness for the artist, it demonstrates his magnificent technique and his command of chiaroscuro effects.

41

GIAMBATTISTA TIEPOLO

## The Immaculate Conception

1767-1769. Oil on canvas,
281 x 155 cm. P363

Tiepolo was commissioned by King
Charles III to paint this picture for
the church of San Pascual in Aran-
juez. Although the subject corre-
sponds to the most deeply-rooted
of Spanish traditions, this very personal work by the Venetian artist
interprets it with an eighteenth-cen-
tury lightness, employing a warm
and delicate colour range and an ele-
gant, formal structure. In accordance with the vision of Saint John
in the *Apocalypse,* the figure of Mary,
crowned with twelve stars, rises
majestically above the globe of the
earth and the serpent, symbol of
evil. Next to her are other Marian
symbols such as the mirror, the lilies
and the palm tree, alluding to her
virtues and to her status as interces-
sor for mankind.

FRANCISCO DE GOYA

## *The Parasol*

1777. Oil on canvas, 104 x 152 cm. P773

This work is a tapestry cartoon – that is to say, the template for the weavers to work from. Goya obtained the commission to paint the cartoons when he first arrived in Madrid thanks to the support of his brother-in-law, Francisco Bayeu. The tapestries were made for the royal palaces at the Royal Tapestry Factory founded in Madrid by Philip V. They show scenes of popular customs and are painted in a joyful, colourful and decorative manner. This cartoon was for a tapestry intended to decorate the dining room of the Prince and Princess of Asturias at the palace of El Pardo, and Goya creates a refined and pleasant scene, very much to the taste of the time, with a classically-influenced pyramidal composition and an exquisite treatment of light.

FRANCISCO DE GOYA

## *The Naked Maja*

1797-1800. Oil on canvas,
98 x 191 cm. P742

At the start of the nineteenth century, *The Naked Maja* and *The Clothed Maja* formed part of the painting collection of Manuel Godoy, Charles IV's first minister, so it is likely that Goya painted them for him, although the exact circumstances of the commission are unknown. Legend has it that they belonged to the Duchess of Alba, and that she may even have been the model, but this thesis is now almost unanimously rejected. Once considered indecent, this nude is an affirmation of the sensuality of a beautiful female body exhibited without mythological or historical pretexts.

# FRANCISCO DE GOYA

## *The Family of Charles IV*

1800. Oil on canvas, 280 x 336 cm. P726

Goya painted this portrait of the royal family shortly after being named First Painter to King Charles IV and Queen María Luisa of Parma, who occupy the centre of the composition, and are surrounded by their children and siblings. Prominent among them is the Prince of Asturias, the future Ferdinand VII, dressed in blue on the left. Behind him, in the background, is a self-portrait of Goya, doubtless a reference to *Las Meninas* and a token of his admiration for Velázquez. At a moment of crisis for the European monarchies, the artist brings great technical and compositional mastery to bear on an image of royal power based on the union of dynasties and the legitimacy of their continuation.

FRANCISCO DE GOYA

## The Third of May, 1808

1814. Oil on canvas, 268 x 347 cm. P749

Along with its companion piece, *The Second of May, 1808, in Madrid,* this work was painted shortly after the end of the Peninsular War waged by the Spaniards and their allies against the armies of Napoleon. Goya shows the execution of the patriots of Madrid who had rebelled against the French invaders the day before, beginning a five-year conflict that provided Goya with the inspiration for numerous paintings, drawings and prints. Among the striking features of the composition are the expressions and gestures of fear and despair among the condemned men, whilst the platoon of anonymous executioners are the image of repression.

FRANCISCO DE GOYA

## *Saturn Devouring his Child*

1821-1823. Mixed technique.
Mural painting transferred to canvas,
143 x 81 cm. P763

This representation of Saturn, the god who devoured his children so that they would not challenge his power, forms part of the series of murals that decorated Goya's house. They are known as the 'Black Paintings' owing to their dark chromatic range and the gloom pervading the scenes. In them, Goya set out along the road to creative freedom. His depictions of expressive deformity and visions of the subconscious became defining elements of modern art. Difficult to interpret as they are, one detects a critical view of the society of his time. Also present are the phantoms of solitude and the fear of death that afflicted the artist during his final years.

EDUARDO ROSALES

## Queen Isabella dictating her Last Will and Testament

1864. Oil on canvas,
290 x 400 cm. P4625

Rosales shows the dying Queen dictating her will in Medina del Campo on 12 October 1504, a few days before her death. Among those with her are a grief-stricken King Ferdinand, their daughter Juana, and Cardinal Cisneros. One of the finest Spanish history paintings, this picture is remarkable for the self-assurance of its drawing, the representation of different textures, and its compositional flair. The Queen is the central focus due to the light and the white tones surrounding her figure. Nineteenth-century painters started to look back to Velázquez after the appearance of this picture, in which Rosales's admiration for the artist is evident.

JOAQUÍN SOROLLA

## *Children on the Beach*

1910. Oil on canvas, 118 x 185 cm. P4648

This painting is a magnificent example of Sorolla's art at the height of his career. He was the creator of a personal style that might be defined as a kind of light-bathed naturalism, purely pictorial in its values. His art is based on the absolute protagonism of light, which sends vibrations through colours and forms defined with broad brushstrokes, as is the case here. No doubt because of his Valencian origin, he always showed a special interest in beach scenes. They allowed him full expression of the qualities which brought him fame and renown during his lifetime. This picture was a personal gift from Sorolla to the Museum of Modern Art, whose collection entered the Prado Museum in 1971.

49

ROMAN WORKSHOP

## *Orestes and Pylades*

c. 10 B.C. White marble.
Height: 161 cm. E28

This work shows Orestes and Pylades, legendary models of friendship, offering a sacrifice to the goddess Artemis, who is represented in the small statuette behind them. This act was meant to purify Orestes for having killed his mother, Clytemnestra, in revenge for the death of his father, Agamemnon. The work belongs to the period of Augustan classicism, and is an excellent example of the artistic eclecticism typical of the first decades of the Roman Empire. Found in Rome in 1623, it later belonged to Queen Christina of Sweden and subsequently to Philip V of Spain, who had it taken to the palace of La Granja de San Ildefonso near Segovia. This is why it is traditionally known as the "San Ildefonso Group".

ANONYMOUS

## *Cup with Golden Mermaid*

Late sixteenth century. Agate,
partially enamelled gold, rubies
and diamonds. 17.5 x 12.5 cm. O1

After the death in 1712 of his father,
the Grand Dauphin of France, son
of Louis XIV, Philip V became the
owner of a collection of precious
objects known as 'The Dauphin's
Treasure'. Fashioned from rock
crystal and hard stones, they are
decorated with exquisite fantasy in
enamels and gems. One that particularly stands out is this cup, possibly
a salt cellar, made up of an agate
bowl supported by a small mermaid,
possibly an allusion to the marine
origins of salt. The figure wears a
headdress of enamelled feathers,
while the arms and torso are orna-
mented with rubies and diamonds.

© of this edition, the text
and the images,
Museo Nacional del Prado

Cover image
Diego Velázquez, *Las Meninas*
(detail), c. 1656
Madrid, Museo Nacional del Prado

Edition
Museo Nacional del Prado

Production
Museo Nacional del Prado Difusión

Translation
Philip Sutton
Elizabeth Mascola

Copy Editor
Natasha Podro

Design
Mikel Garay

Layout
Jesús García Serrano

Prepress
Lucam

Printer
Brizzolis, arte en gráficas

ISBN 978-84-8480-136-8
NIPO 555-07-025-8
D.L. M-52790-2007

GOBIERNO DE ESPAÑA   MINISTERIO DE CULTURA

MUSEO NACIONAL
DEL **PRADO**

**PEFC**

PEFC/14-38-00082
Paper from sustainably
managed forests.
For more information:
www.pefc.org

11-11